T0365807

a pearl's promise

the mystery of me

by Jennifer Toomy

To order additional copies of this book, contact:
Xlibris
844-714-8691
www.Xlibris.com
Orders@Xlibris.com

ISBN: Softcover   978-1-4257-8659-5
             Hardcover   978-1-4257-8663-2

Print information available on the last page

Rev. date: 05/02/2024

a pearl's promise

I was walking along the river in Richmond feeling like I had let the best opportunity I'd had to make myself happy slip away. Tears were in my eyes. I'd lost my best friend, the man I'd loved...but not enough to confront the negative things in my life. I had settled for the way things were. I was too afraid. I had just kept living...and here I was. I'd lost sight of what mattered.

And then my cell phone rang. I sat down on the sidewalk. It was him...

He offered me his trust... He offered me hope...not the hope of getting him back...it was the hope that maybe I could use what we'd learned together to help me and my daughter find, to live, the lives we wanted.

Everyday after that conversation, I did one thing to move closer to what I wanted for me and for my daughter. This was the gift he'd given to me...his trust, his love, his friendship. He uncovered the promise I held inside for too long.

That is when he offered me "grains of sand."

When she was born, he was the first to hold her. He started writing the letters...letters about grains of sand...how an oyster turns the irritation caused by a grain of sand into a beauty[ful] pearl. The letters to my daughter are based on the natural process of a pearl, a grain of sand sparking transformation and growth, into one of nature's most beauty[ful] gems, a pearl, the only gem brought forth by, created within, a living be[ing]...other than our children, of course.

The first letter was about the grains of sand, then beauty, how you needed to have beauty to be beauty[ful]...then came true[th], and moment and wonder...and they kept coming...

This is the story of how unexpected things in our lives can be made into something beauty[ful]... even myself...and especially my daughter. Lives can be lived in this simple way...our moments in life strung together by the strands of feel, beauty, trust, wonder....if only we could hold onto them. People have asked us over and over again, how do we help our children hold onto these intangibles of feel and wonder and beauty?

By living that way ourselves.

grains of sand

I offer these letters to you
with the simple lesson of a pearl
to be who you are,
discover who you are meant to be

the value of diamonds in cutting off flaws,
with sharp edges,
to be seen but not held,
to be envied and stand alone

the promise you share with me
promises born as grains of sand
sand that gives birth to inspiration
nature gently weaves of you and me
crystals and silk and beauty
layer upon layer

a perfect fit of pearl and oyster
of parent and child, of you and me
in trust and wonder of ourselves
free of envy or sharp edges

your beauty illuminated like a strand of perfection
one pearl resting alongside another, you next to me...
like sand between toes
nature called us to work
one crystal at a time, silk spun into trust
to hug the crystals yet to come
to allow you to grow
towards the pearl you might be

being a pearl

"be where you are"
is where we'll begin
to help you create
the THERE you dream of

the stillness inside you
the maker of moments

the rhythm of Nature
lifts you aloft
where the earth still believes you
and the world can't deceive you

snapshots we take
as you paint your portrait
are the stories we form
into powerful crystals

the hugs and smiles
the touches and dreams
illuminate layers
with wonder and well[th]

the silk of friendships
weave the crystals together
the pad you'll return to
in the love you remember

being a pearl

she calls you to play
so you learn the lessons
of The Game with No Name
that I could not teach you
playing together
yet learned on your own
embraced in the moment
that shines from your smile

energy informed, doing your work
in finding and freeing, feeding and following
powered by feel
the feel that's all yours

me

the break of the waves, the phase of the moon
meant fall was at hand, summer leaving too soon
the grains of sand, in salt water, drifting
alight on my feet, against my skin, sifting

atop my foot, two grains came to rest
this made them special, they were the best
I wondered what differed, made them unique
did they have a purpose, one they would seek?

that is the question, what makes me "me?"
the eyes and soul with which only I see
the hands and the voice with which only I speak
will they be strong, or choose to be meek?

grains of sand huddled en masse
some of them fused and turned into glass
others await the ebb and the flow
for the tide to take them wherever they go

what of this sand that's stuck to my skin
what kind of life are they to begin
somehow different than all of the rest
were they to fulfill a destiny's quest?

me

is that how it is that I came to be
is that how it is, that there is a "me"
my play[ce] in this dance came without invitation
does that make my life a mere imitation?

this is the gift you and I share
a gift to those accepting the dare
the gift of the sand on my foot uninvited
a gift hard to see, like a love unrequited

we are the stuff of life unexpected
from life of the average we have defected
the stories they tell us, feel a bit incomplete
minds that seek answers, with questions replete

but here is the true[th], one thing I can trust
a pearl is a promise of how life is thrust
from a grain of sand misplaced into beauty
we must accept our own unique duty

the wonder of us, of those uninvited
unexpected we were, when on earth we alighted
mothers make magic, from sand comes a pearl
blessed by the women whose promise unfurls

me

asleep in their arms, they gave us our start
a play^{ce} to return to, a play^{ce} in their hearts
they gave us our play^{ce}, a shared history
and they told of a secret, a grand mystery

before we could speak, before we both knew
they were giving me "me," giving you "you"
ensuring our wonder was folded and packed
unconditional love, for nothing we lacked

something unspoken in two grains of sand
a something we feel, we must understand
something we've be^{en}, no one else ever knows
a be and be^{come}, only a pearl ever goes

These letters to you, a lesson I'll share
a story untold, of paths who knows where
and when "moments" happen, I hope you will see
what you feel incomplete, is your heart's only key

the path we must take, a trail in the sand
marked by the stars, not seen easy on land
taken before, washed cleaned by the tide
a path made alone, from something inside

me

the pearl's promise to you, the same as to me
the wonder to question the mystery of me
let others stay huddled, forming the beach
we'll see what we're made of, what's in our reach

one thing I'll ask you, my only request
when "I" comes a'knocking that you do your best
remember the women that gave us our start
remember the women put "me" in our hearts

"I" is the diamond, with flaws cut away
hoping with envy that people will pay
but "me" is the pearl, handmade by the mother
"me" is the beauty, no judgment of others

Whatever you feel, whatever you think
"me" is the key, the crystalline link
to what you have be^{en}, will be, and be^{come}
the mysterious "me," your final freedom

youth

words of old age, a toll that's been rung
those who might say, youth's wasted on young
how would you know, time's perpetual wish
youth will be served, silver spoon, golden dish

so why write this letter, why take the time
to explain what's as simple as rhythm and rhyme
one morning you'll wake and no longer play
I'll wonder with sorrow, who's taken our days

here is my lesson, so please don't forget
this lesson if lost, a life of regret

it's you next to me, investing in wonder
your hand held in mine, laughing off blunders
what is this youth you have that we covet?
it's knowing yourself and learning to love it

the stillness you know, abed in your home
and taking it with you, wherever you roam
the power of waves, riding sandbar to shore
childhood friends, their knock on your door

youth

where does it go, a wish we might keep
a seed that you sow, and the magic it reaps
the best trick of all, the mysterious "me"
not a play^{ce} in your past, but a play^{ce} yet to be

you are the wonder, the beauty I see
the talent of youth is setting you free
trusting yourself, your own set of skills
to follow your dream, whatever it wills

the Game with No Name, played so stories evolve
from sands into pearls, the cycle revolves
turn off the clock, set watches aside
the rhythm of you is all to abide

its not in the fame, not found in the money
it's keeping alive, tooth fairies and bunnies
invite in tomorrow, keep open the past
in youth and the "moment," old age cannot last.

moment

worry not
when time takes the light from the day
or the leaves start to fall
from the tree to the earth
don't worry in silence
of things left undone
or wonder too late
of what went unsaid

from day into night
then back into day
take hold of my hand
I'll show you the way
past the monsters of time
trolls under the bridge
to play^{ces} called "moments"
where you and I'll play

"my moment" defined
in stillness and space
when be^{en}, be, be^{come}
move smoothly as one

a life lived in moments
a story well told
of experiences pure
feels free
of the clock's ticking

moment

moments are well[th]
held together by silk
revealing beauty
held in wonder
when the mystery of me
solves itself
if only for a second
my "promise" fulfilled

my moment
the measure of my experience
living free
feel transcending time

wonder*ful*

wonder's a feel, a call to your soul
to discover your play^ce, to question your role
to seek the divine, to find something higher
music that moves you, awe that inspires

wonder's the waves, the wind of attraction
moves you towards beauty, not ugly distractions
wonder's the questions, curiosity pure
the mysteries of life, your heart's simple stir

your smile and hug remind me to wonder
of the power in Nature, of lightning and thunder
of how we're connected, of how we're the same
in the promise we're born with, in the Game with No Name

wonder's the gift, the source of all movement
wonder's the power ensuring improvement
a tap on your shoulder, a feel you should follow
into the woods and down to the hollow

where Nature awaits to give you the tools
to find your own beauty priced above jewels
wonder's the force that blazes the trail
gives you the strength to live your own tale

wonder*ful*

wonder's the song you feel beat in your heart
a rhythm to dance to, your journey to start
wonder's the hunger, life's ultimate thirst
for beauty and true[th], for what's best and what's first

so wonder aloud and I'll share the stories
of adventures and treasures, of bountiful quarries
to answer your questions with questions my own
together we'll travel, not wander alone

so wonder in silence, let no one intrude
on you[th] that is yours, that playing exudes
so wonder in stillness of the beauty inside you
a beauty you feel, of friends right beside you

wonder's the call, a simple attraction
to learn to let go of what is distracting
to hold onto awe, of your promise inside
to find the play[ce] you'll choose to reside

wonder aloud wherever you are,
and I will come find you by the sun and the stars
wonder in silence and you'll come to see
wonder[ful] happens where wonder roams free

beautyful

a question for we, how is beauty defined?
in the mystery of me or we grains when refined?
your eyes look to me, I say I don't know
where should we look and where should we go?

"what to take with us?"
"we'll need wonder and trust"
you give me a smile and that let's me know
they're already with you wherever you go

that is the answer, the beauty I see
your moves like a dancer, and how they touch me

do you feel the same feel when you look in a mirror?
my youth reappears, a picture now clearer
beauty that's yours not so easy to be
when the beauty of others is all that you see

beauty's a language one learns before birth
how nature attracts us to venture the earth
signaled by feel with wonder and trust
before words ever spoken, a grammar of us

b e a u t y^{ful}

the Game with No Name wants "we" to play
before tv and movies lead us astray
beauty remembered, turned into power
and you hand it to me, a beauty^{ful} flower

my stillness of moment you see like a mirror
now it is you who feels beauty clearer
a flower, a gift, in me what you see
beauty when one is made of these three

our laugh and our hug are letting me know
beauty's to be given where ever you go
the songs we sing, the music we hear
beauty, the language, of what we hold dear

we've answered our question that beauty is us
like the into-me-key, to turn beauty takes trust
but you can't keep what you feel is lost
my promise to you, my love at no cost

the work to be done, "we" closer to beauty^{ful}
your own sense of beauty, keep trusting and dutiful
beauty, a calling to reach out to another
not given "away," what we give to each other

true*th*

what does it mean, it's the ultimate question?
the best I can say, it's nature's suggestion
what I can share, for me, still a riddle
an answer not found living life in the middle

discovering life as Nature designed
in the be^{ing} you are, the role you're assigned
don't get me wrong, I've not seen the plan
of Nature's intentions and the future of man

trueth is a search conducted with trust
trueth is the moment you find what you must
expanding yourself in the way of the pearl
the wisdom of women and the wonder of girls

Is trueth in the journey or unknown destination?
maybe trueth's found in sheer fascination
expressed in the building with crystals and silk
grown into pearls the color of milk

trueth is the trust in "moments" that silence
the ticking of time and fear's inner violence

trueth is the "stories" written inside you
not the teller of tales who lies right beside you

trueth

true[th] is the beauty compelling you nearer
not beauty you're told to see in the mirror

true[th] is the mastery of you[th] and its skills
not the indifference most adulthood instills

true[th] is the music, the sounds that inform
not the noise of the world, not the call to conform

the feel of a hug conveying the true[th]
that smile you smile that's missing a tooth

stillness and silence, beyond empty spaces,
sweetest music of all, these internal play[ces]
where you[th] reveals true[th], then sets you free
to find and behold your into-me-key

kind^{ness}

the touch of your hand, the things that you've said
the smile in your voice, how you sleep in your bed
the love in my heart, the kind that is timeless
there's hope for the world, because of your kind^{ness}

so I offer these words, in the form of this letter
to hold onto kind^{ness}, to make this world better
I'll tell you the tale of on old shopping cart
once left in the lot of the neighborhood mart

a story of life, what goes unobserved
Once shiny and new, the cart meant to serve
Let's you and I watch, to see what occurs
to see all these people when kind^{ness} demurs

day after day, they come and they go
some of them rushing, the world moves too slow
So they empty the bags, cell phone in their ears
shove kids in the cars, from new model years

you and I watch from the car where we park
as carts are abandoned, and the drivers embark
by the end of the day, carts looking like litter
and people who dodge them, grow angry and bitter

23

kind^{ness}

you ask me about it, wonder aloud
why not return them, are people too proud
the best I can say is people are busy
they rush at a pace that's leaving them dizzy

you get out of the car, take a cart to the rack
and smile at me and I smile back
you answer your question with such common sense
I can only describe it as pure elegant⁵

we live in a world that uses words freely
"love," "nice,' and "dreams" from mouths that are mealy
the thing about kids, they still cherish and "like"
its friends, and ice cream, even a bike

and the hope of the earth, in a world that seems blind
is the promise of children, who choose to be kind
Don't say it at all if you can't say it nice
but I have some better, old fashioned advice

say nothing at all, just try to be kind
in the things that you do, the way life is refined
thank you and please, hold the door for each other
reach out your hand to the needs of another

kindness

as we sit and we talk, we see kindness itself
the homeless man walks, with a pride holds himself
he washes a cart, his belongings beside it
he treats the old cart as if gold were inside it

he washes it clean, and then wipes it dry
he gives it a push, he gives it a try
he talks as he walks as if it can hear him
unaware of the shoppers, of those who would fear him

the shoppers and folks who slam them around
who leave them to roll when on slanted ground
too busy, too lazy, too damned all important
they're left in the lot, when care's been exported

but here is a man with nothing to lose
the man takes care of the cart he will use
I see in your smile, that you get the point
the rest of the world he need not anoint

remember this story, remember inside you
that kindness can happen to the person beside you
if you'll live life in moments, seek kindness above duty
even carts in a lot are containers of beauty

feel... feelings

we'll sit in the sand, let the sea touch our toes
awaiting the day, the one each of us knows
a summer of sadness, that takes you to college
in search of the true[th], in search of some knowledge

maybe the moment comes sooner than that
when your heart seems to split, your mood sinking flat
leaving behind your family and friends
trails to be cut, what's familiar soon ends

"It doesn't seem fair" your tears will sing out
the comfort of home gives way to some doubt
this is the letter of a lesson that hurts
a future is calling and the past must avert

this is the moment they go separate ways
trails to be blazed through uncomfortable days
feelings gain strength, while "feel," it subsides
but this is the moment to commit to and ride

subtle the difference of feel next to feelings
of what might be[come] and the past might be stealing
feel is the "moment" of beauty and wonder
feelings just memories of triumph and blunder

27

feel... feelings

you'll walk out the door, a look over your shoulder
and your mother will cry, "I just want to hold her"
your feelings will hurt for what seems to be lost
but you must keep on walking or suffer the cost

you won't understand that HERE is no longer
in the home you have made where feelings are stronger
feelings of doubt with THERE not so clear
The trick is to know, that feel defines HERE

HERE is the playce you capture through feel
where feelings of past must bow down and kneel
feelings, just memories of feel used before
we readied you well to walk through the door

the lesson of youth is that feel is a skill
forging the dreams that follow your will
the lesson of age, one not always learned
that been is not be, new life must be earned

feel is the compass to know where you are
feelings, our stories, the heart's Northward Star
How do I say this, with words, not just chatter
feel is the call that gives feelings their matter

feel... feelings

what do you feel awake in the morning?
do you look to the past in sorrow, with mourning?
or do you look to the sky, to the birds and the bees
for the moment, the chance, the THERE you should seize?

one leads you forth, and the other reminds you
our moments together so the future will find you
Follow the feel to the play^ce of that key
wherever you go, you and me be^come we

remember that feelings are the stories of us
the well^th that you carry, not ashes and dust
the power of feelings comes from knowing the past
but feelings without feel keeps the nets never cast

doing our best is the best we can do
setting the stage for the "me" that is you
please don't forget that the games we did play
honing HERE's skills, not a past you obey

finding the feel is where you will start
freeing the feel, the most difficult part
one thing is certain, an absolute given
feel maps the trail of a life that needs living

feel... feelings

feelings are memories of what we have be^{en}
feelings the dreams, what might happen when
but feel is the song of what now stands inside us
wonder, trueth, beauty, the friends right beside us

when the feel that is yours, you happen to find
give be^{en} a last look, as the past slips behind
please set it free, wave a simple goodbye
follow the feel to the play^{ce} you can fly

time will come soon when we'll sit on the beach
we'll always be close, our touch within reach
that's the pearl's promise, a bond never broken
our trust and belief, no words need be spoken

be^en, be, be^come

I'll tell you a story I'd like to share
a story for those who love and who dare
the triplets tale of life spent together
living inside us, always, forever

it's not of your past, not of tomorrow
the feelings you carry of joy and of sorrow
who you are now is what makes us "be"
here in this play^ce, a moment you're free

these triplets they fight, in need of attention
holding our promise in a form of detention
missing the past, a future of worry
leads us to live our lives in a hurry

Where have you gone, who have you be^en?
we all have regrets we play over again
what we have done, what we still feel
be is the promise, the past tries to steal

be^en has it's play^ce, one seat at the table
it's purpose to teach, us to enable
to live in the here, with wisdom instill
to be who we are, to strengthen our will

be^{en}, be, be^{come}

be^{en}, too often, is love kept inside
never set free, behind walls it resides
frozen in fear by the pain and the hurts
of those unrequited, of those who desert

remember the stories, the ones that you wrote
of the moments you lived, how love made you float
love is what matters, the actions that show it
before triplets conflicted, calling fear to erode it

be^{en}, be, and be^{come}
who knows where they're from
when the three join together, working as one
life seems so simple, can be lots of fun

be is the key, the link to the others
be is the key to finding "anothers"
the people who matter, whom your heart ought to know
the play^{ces} that call you, where your heart wants to go

wonder and beauty, feel and what's trueth
happen in be, and keep worry aloof
there is no be^{en}, if be has gone missing
stuck in the past, of those we miss kissing

be^en, be, be^come

the power of be to let promise unfold
and what of tomorrow, what does it hold?
hold onto be^en, for what it inspires
dream of be^come, to find your desires

be^en, be, and be^come
taken together, more than their sum
a symphony written, it's playing inside
music that powers life's wonder^ful ride

work must begin, starting HERE, go to THERE
a journey that goes wherever you dare
a past and a future, full of the promise
be is the power of the life that's upon us

the
GAME
with no name

as morning broke, with sleep in your eyes
a question you asked, took me by surprise
"why must you work? why can't we play
why won't I see you, until night steals the day?"

I knew of an answer, the words not so easy
why miss the sun or the winds blowing breezy?
it comes down to work, and knowing the power
found in the blossom of a beauty^{ful} flower

so I'd grab your soul and we'd go see
all that surrounds us, working to be
we step into morning, our hearts on a tether
standing in silence, in wonder, together

there in the grass, is my cat named Boo
we take time to watch, to see what she'll do
the pieces of paper she took from the house
pretending somehow it's a white tasty mouse

Boo leaps in the air, honing her skills
and that ball of paper now does what she wills
so when the time comes, she'll know she can do it
whatever life takes, she'll know to get through it

the
GAME
with no name

up in the air, birds circle serenely
rising, then falling, riding winds cleanly
how do I tell you this is their work
that keeps them alive, keeps them alert

why do we work, I haven't an answer
when so many people treat it like cancer
and then I see it, a question much better
that is the point of this particular letter

why do you play? I ask you aloud
because I'm a kid, you answer so proud
in the moment of play, what is it you do
keeping you focused, your aim so true?

the more that you play, the better you get
the better you get, the less you will fret
in whatever you play , a HERE and a THERE
moving between these is the work we're aware

the Game with No Name, that special way
work is done best when we do it with play
pay no attention, who see work as a grind
see home as escape, just a play^{ce} to unwind

the
GAME
with no name

Boo and the birds, the clouds and the sea
do the best work to feel the most free
it is choosing the work, the way it gets done
that makes all the difference, makes your Game fun

so I go to work, to play and to grow
to do my own work in a way that I'll know
when we're together it is me that I'll bring
play to our fullest, live our own special thing

one day you'll know enough to decide
that play is the work, the work done inside
moves you closer to THERE, your special design
play is the work, how "you" is refined

whatever you do, whatever you choose
play with No Name, a game you can't lose
as long as you play and follow the feel
life's at your will, something no one can steal

the Game with No Name, played so stories evolve
from sands into pearls, the cycle revolves
compete to improve in the Game you will play
wellth will be yours, and youth made to stay

37

wellth

wonder is calling, the music of youth
calling you forward in search of your trueth
the beauty you feel, the song you can hear
take one step at a time, breathe away fear

a rhythm to follow, to free and to feed
a nurturing dance reveals what you need
we'll call it wellth, the skills of the promise
to go where you choose, confront what's upon us

when you were born, it was all you could see
the world was no bigger than that tiny "me"
waiting for others to take care of your needs
loving and growing, your only deeds

one day you'll awake to the chatter and noise
where life is no longer you playing with toys
it can be scary and a little confusing
but listen to me and we'll make it amusing

it's life's invitation to develop your skill
to discover the promise that nature instills
here in this letter, the best that I can
to tell of the wellth that rests in your hands

well ᵗʰ

you have what you need, youth is sufficient
to move through a world that's growing deficient
wellth is the you increasing your power
still feeling the sun, to taste a spring shower

wellth is the moments you're weaving together
forming a pearl of crystals and tethers

wellth is the memories that make up the stories
of who you've be^{come}, transcending past glories

wellth can be found in the how and the why
wellth's not the sum of the things you can buy

wellth is the wonder that calls you to beauty
wellth is the power of your personal duty

wellth is the wisdom of youth gaining knowledge
not found in the pressures of going to college

wellth is the skill with which you can speak
to those who are fluent in the life that you seek

well th

wellth is in showing the beauty within
when ignorance worries where to begin

wellth is in be^{ing} the friend who can listen
to whose magic is lost and no longer glistens

wellth starts with "me" instructed by youth
follows wonder to beauty then into trueth
measured in moments, wellth transcends time
wellth is the skills of your promise refined

wellth is in gathering, then using the tools
that turns sand into pearl, biology's jewel
wellth is your life, the pursuit of living
wellth is the act, the power in giving

well th

My life as a woman, as a mother, means each day creating wellth for myself and my daughter—not looking for someone to take care of us, but to care about ourselves. It means getting better a little bit every day, fulfilling my own promise—of myself...to myself.

What have I learned? I've learned that wellth is about remembering the skills of youth—wonder and play and unconditional love. I remembered how free I felt as a child, how I used that freedom to learn and grow without anyone telling me to do that.

I've learned that wellth is about seeing and living the mystery in myself, those unknown parts of me that called out to me for so long, a call I had never answered, and tried to ignore. Wellth is embracing that mystery, confronting the fear.

I've learned that wellth is the passion for living my life, how time disappears when I am doing those things I love, how moments are more powerful than clocks and calendars.

I've learned that wellth is found in my ability to make those moments last longer by staying in them, by slowing down, holding the hug a little longer...and sharing that stillness with my daughter.

Wellth is the stories of my past I want to remember, the stories I want to tell my daughter. It is the pictures of my past woven together into a portrait of who I have be^{en}, and a celebration of who I am. Wellth is the dreams of what I can be and the tools to be^{come} that.

Wellth is wonder and beauty and power and trueth and moments.

Wellth is the skills to use them to wake up each day knowing how I want to feel and how to create that feel. Wellth is going to sleep every night exhausted from play...and like a child, dreaming about what I am going to play tomorrow.

Printed in the United States
by Baker & Taylor Publisher Services